xBiog Orr.B May.J
May, Julian.
Bobby Orr, star on ice.

BOBBY ORR
STAR ON ICE

BOBBY ORR
STAR ON ICE

by Julian May

Published by Crestwood House, Inc., Mankato, Minnesota 56001. Published simultaneously in Canada by J. M. Dent and Sons, Ltd. Library of Congress Catalog Card Number: 73-80422. International Standard Book Number: 0-913940-02-X. Text copyright © 1973 by Julian May Dikty. Illustrations copyright © 1973 by Crestwood House, Inc. All rights reserved. No part of this book may be reproduced in any form without written permission from the publisher, except for brief passages included in a review. Printed in the United States of America.

Designed by William Dichtl

Crestwood House, Inc., Mankato, Minn. 56001

PHOTOGRAPHIC CREDITS

Boston Bruins: 15, 25; Information Canada Photothèque (M. Senak): 9; Maclean-Hunter Publishing Co. Ltd.: 18, 20, 23; Michael Philip Manheim: 2, 6; Oshawa Generals: 14, 17, 19; Publication Associates: 10, 12-13; United Press International: 24, 27, 28, 29, 32, 35, 36, 37, 38-39, 40, 41, 42, 43, 44, 45; Wide World Photos: 30, 31, 34, 46, 47. Cover: Wide World Photos.

BOBBY ORR
STAR ON ICE

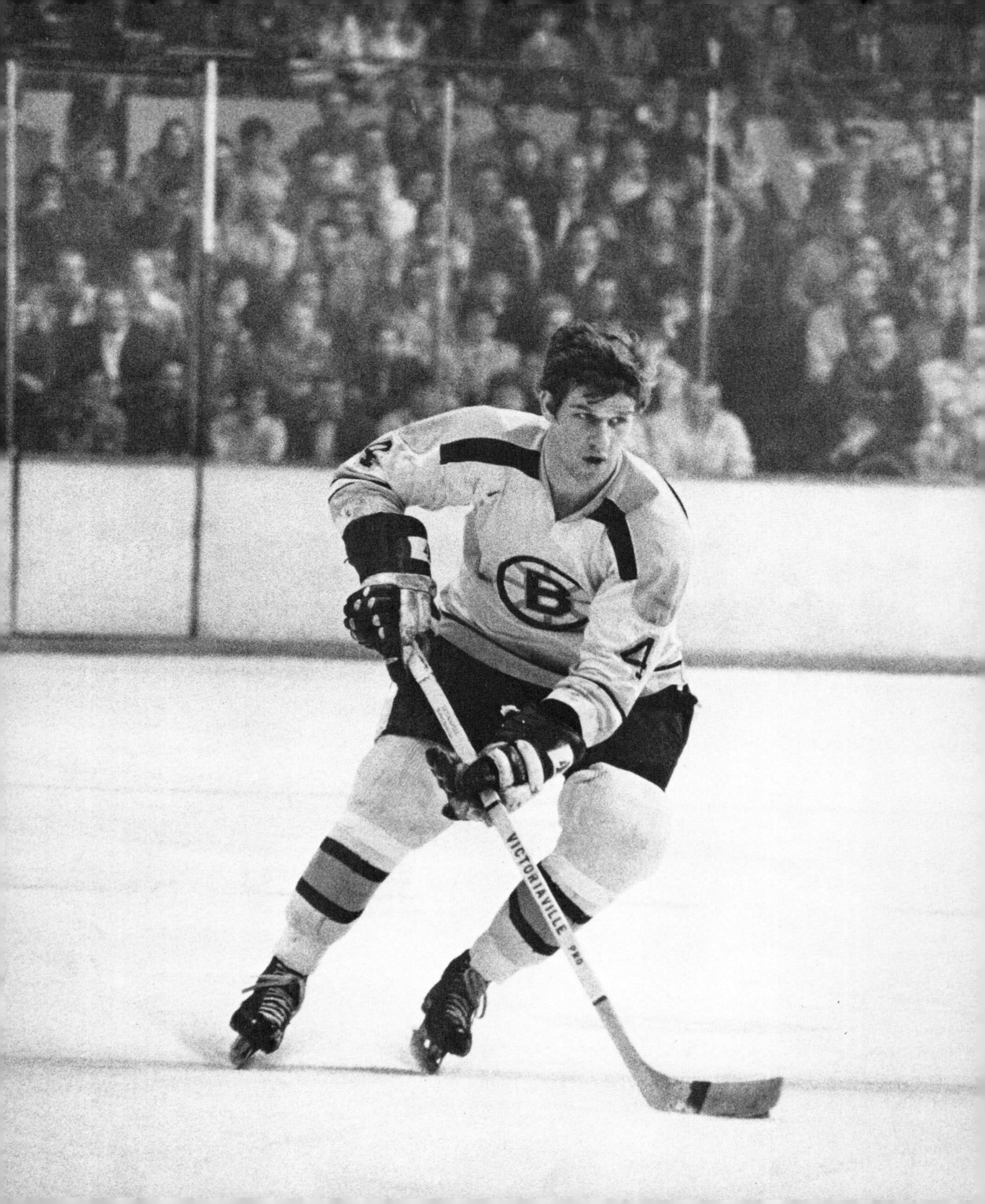
VICTORIAVILLE PRO

The winters are cold in Parry Sound, Ontario. The icy wind blows off Lake Huron and there is almost always several feet of snow.
    The boys of the town clean the snow off the frozen Seguin River. All winter long they play hockey.

In 1952, four-year-old Bobby Orr got his first pair of skates and joined the older boys. At first, he could hardly keep his ankles from bending. The other boys laughed as he wobbled along.

But soon Bobby learned to skate well. When he was five, he could keep the puck away from much older boys. Sometimes his father, Doug Orr, would come down to watch his little son play. He smiled as Bobby went sailing through a yelling crowd, handling his stick like an expert.

"Bobby is a natural," Doug Orr thought. He remembered his own youth, when he played so well that a scout from the Bruins wanted to give him a try-out. But World War II had come along—and Doug Orr joined the Navy. When the war was over, he was too old for pro hockey. But he still loved the game. And he was glad that Bobby seemed to love it, too.

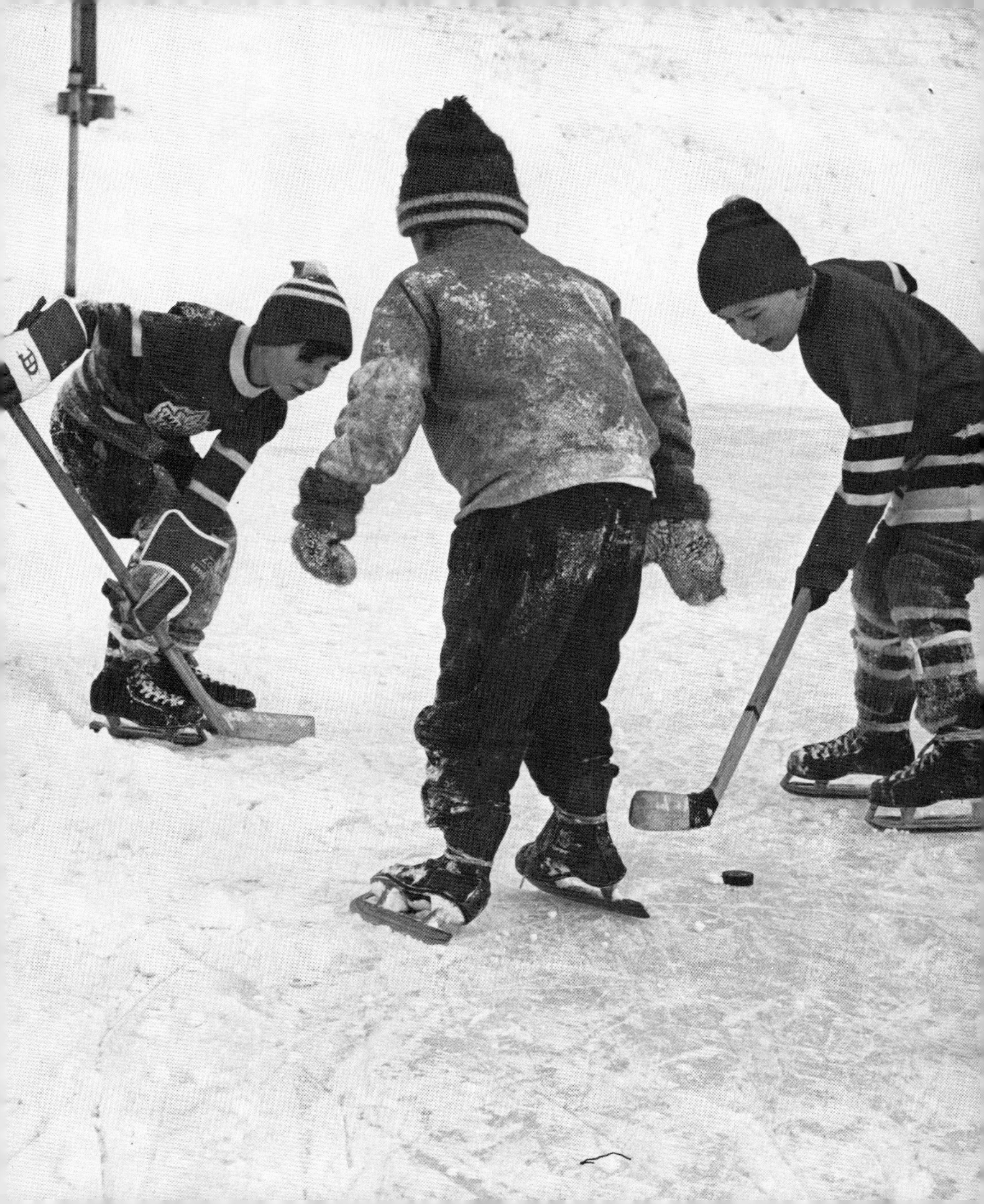

The Orr family home in Parry Sound, Ontario, where Bobby lived as a boy. Bobby was the third of five children. His father worked as a packer in a local explosives factory.

10

Parry Sound had a Minor Hockey Association with an indoor rink. Bobby began playing for the Minor Squirt Division team when he was still in kindergarten. As he grew older, he dominated each division he played in. He was a small boy—but he starred at defense, a position usually given to the biggest and strongest kids.

The Parry Sound teams were coached by Bucko MacDonald, who had once played for the Toronto Maple Leafs. MacDonald helped Bobby to become an outstanding defenseman. When Bobby was nine, he won Ontario's Most Valuable Pee Wee award. When he was twelve, he began to dream of becoming a pro.

In winter, the Seguin River next to the Orr house (arrow) froze, making a perfect hockey arena.

That year, 1960, the Parry Sound team qualified for the Bantam Division championship tournament. The boys traveled to the town of Gananoque, Ontario, where the tournament was to be held.

Bobby played against boys who were two years older. Nevertheless, he seemed to play rings around the others. His team lost the playoff, 1-0, but Bobby was voted Most Valuable Player in the tournament.

And without knowing it, he had also taken his first step toward becoming a professional hockey player. Four scouts from the Boston Bruins had watched him play. They knew at once that he was something special. And they were determined to grab him for Boston.

A friendly official from the Boston Bruins came to Parry Sound with great news. The Boston team would become the sponsor of Parry Sound's junior hockey program. The Bruins were ready to contribute money to buy new equipment. Everybody wondered why a faraway hockey team should be so generous. Before long, the secret was out: the Bruins wanted Bobby Orr.

It may seem strange that an NHL team would be so interested in a 12-year-old boy. But the Boston Bruins were slipping. They had no good young players coming up. Other NHL teams had their stars and talented youngsters—but not Boston. They had finished fifth in the 1959-60 season. The next year they would take up housekeeping in hockey's cellar.

13

Wren Blair, the man who snared young Bobby Orr for the Boston Bruins organization, was the general manager of the Oshawa Generals hockey team, a Canadian Junior A farm club in the amateur Ontario Hockey Association.

Bobby Orr, young as he was, was a hope for the future. According to the rules, the Bruins could sign Bobby to their Junior A farm team when he was 14. But other hockey clubs were interested in the boy, too. Scouts for Montreal, Toronto, Detroit, and Chicago also began sniffing around Parry Sound.

The next year, Bobby played on the Midget team. All through the season, the Orr family was visited by a friendly Bruin official named Wren Blair. He managed the Bruin's Junior A team at Oshawa, Ontario. He worked very hard getting Doug and Arva Orr to agree to send Bobby to the Bruins' junior tryout camp.

Milt Schmidt, coach of the Bruins at the time of Bobby Orr's discovery, later became general manager of the team and built the Bruins into champions.

Lynn Patrick, former general manager of the Boston Bruins, helped discover Bobby Orr at Gananoque.

Bobby's parents finally agreed to let him try out in August, 1962. But they were afraid that Bobby was still too young and too small for the rough-and-tumble play of the older boys.

They need not have worried. Bobby was the smallest defenseman at the hockey camp. But he was also the best.

Now Wren Blair began to push the Orrs hard. He told Doug and Arva that their son would someday be a great hockey star—*if* he got the proper training. He had to play with a Junior A team such as Blair's Oshawa Generals in order to develop properly. If he stayed in Parry Sound, he would learn bad habits because he was much better than all the other players.

The Orrs hesitated. Oshawa was a large city, 150 miles from Parry Sound, down near Toronto. Bobby was too young to live away from home. He would be lonesome. And what would happen to his schoolwork?

After a lot of discussion, Mr. and Mrs. Orr agreed to let Bobby play for Oshawa. Wren Blair had to promise to let Bobby continue to live at home. His father would drive him to the games in Oshawa.

If play was too rough, or if Bobby's schoolwork suffered, he would have the right to pull out.

Bobby Orr in the uniform of the Oshawa Generals.

Coach Jim Cherry of the Generals gives 16-year-old Bobby some instructions during practice.

Bobby Orr was the smallest player on the Oshawa team. Because he lived 150 miles away, he would have no time to practice with the others. Some of the other players grumbled about this—until they saw how Bobby performed on the ice.

He was very fast and he could change direction as easily as a fish. Hockey is a rough game and some of the larger boys did their best to crush Oshawa's little defenseman. But Bobby learned to take it and dish it out. In his first season, he scored 13 goals as well as proving himself to be agile in the defense. He made the second All-Star Team.

Bobby (white jersey) in action for Oshawa.

The next year, Bobby's parents decided he was old enough to live away from home during the hockey season. The manager of the Generals promised Doug and Arva that Bobby would live with families that would treat him as their own son. And this is the way it turned out. Hockey practice and schoolwork left him little time to feel homesick—and no time at all to get into trouble.

Out on the ice, he continued to develop his unusual talents. The Bruins' management watched him closely. Back in Boston, the fans stayed loyal while the Bruins finished last for three years in a row. "Just wait until Bobby Orr gets here!" people said.

Amazing as it seems, the Boston Bruins were waiting for Bobby Orr to grow up so that he could save the team.

MACLEAN'S 15¢

Canada's National Magazine February 20 1965

How hockey's hottest 16-year-old is groomed for stardom

Bobby Orr: a fan's-eye view. Has Boston captured the NHL's next super-star?

During his second season with Oshawa, Bobby set a league scoring record for defensemen—30 goals. During his third season, when he was 16, he played so well that a national magazine put his picture on the cover with the headline:

HAS BOSTON CAPTURED THE NHL'S NEXT SUPERSTAR?

Bobby scored 34 goals and made 59 assists that season. Despite the great pressure, he was getting better and better. Boston fans could hardly wait for the critical day—March 20, 1966—when Bobby would be 18 and eligible for an NHL contract.

During the 1965-66 season, Bobby scored 37 goals and 60 assists. Excitement in Boston rose to a pitch of hysteria. Led by Bobby Orr, the Oshawa Generals won the Junior A championship and the Eastern Canada Junior championship. All that was left was the Memorial Cup finals, which decided the top Junior team in Canada.

The Oshawa Generals faced the Edmonton Oil Kings in the Memorial Cup best-of-seven series. Unfortunately, Bobby had pulled a groin muscle. The manager of the Boston Bruins, Hap Emms, was afraid Bobby might injure himself seriously if he played in the series. All he could think of were the future needs of Boston. He said:

"That boy is not going to play!"

But Bobby wanted his team, the Generals, to win the Memorial Cup. In spite of the pain, he said he would play. And his father backed him up.

The Generals trailed the series, 3-2. Bobby went out on the ice and did his best to win that critical sixth game. The audience could see that he was in pain— and many of them wept as crippled Bobby tried to stem the Oil Kings' advance. But the Generals lost the game and the Cup.

When Bobby left the ice, the fans gave him a standing ovation.

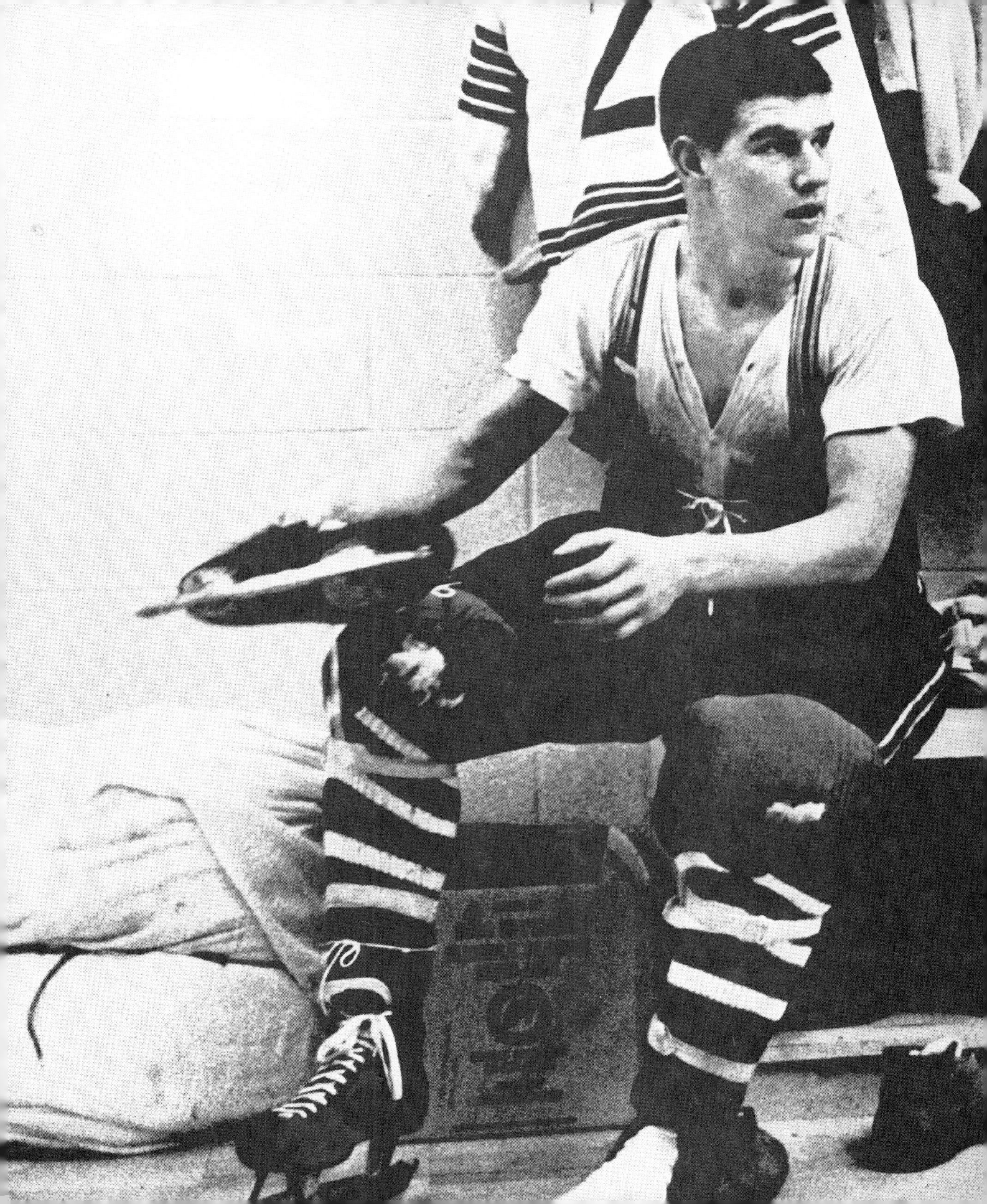

Boston rookies line up at their first practice session in 1966. *Left to right:* Joe Watson, Wayne Connolly, Dick Cherry, Ross Lonsberry, Bobby Orr, Ted Hodgson.

Now it was time for Boston to offer Bobby a pro contract. Everybody expected that he would join the team at once. But in 1966, not even star hockey players were very highly paid. Hap Emms offered Bobby a contract that called for a very low salary.

Doug and Bobby turned the offer down. Magazines and newspapers had written articles calling Bobby a "million-dollar player." If Bobby Orr was going to make a fortune for the owners of the Boston Bruins, it was only right that he get a salary that reflected his talent.

Doug and Bobby needed expert advice. They turned to an old friend, a Toronto lawyer named Alan Eagleson. He agreed to be Bobby's agent.

At first, Hap Emms refused to even talk to Eagleson. Then he said that Bobby might as well give in and take the low salary. No other NHL team could sign him.

Eagleson said: "What if Bobby spends the next season in amateur hockey? He could play with the National Hockey Team of Canada. He's young. He can afford to wait another year."

But could Boston?

Emms was trapped. There was no way he could go home again without Bobby Orr. Boston had built the boy up too high with the fans.

Emms finally had to agree to pay Bobby a salary four times as much as the first offer. Then Bobby signed the contract that made him a Boston Bruin.

It was an important day in pro hockey. Not only because Boston acquired a superstar—but also because Bobby's salary inspired other hockey players to demand more money. Within a short time, hockey players would no longer be low men on the totem pole of pro athletics. They would be paid as much as football, baseball, or basketball stars.

Leighton "Hap" Emms, who was Bruins general manager during Bobby Orr's first year with the team.

Training camp was confusing to Bobby. He was so good that the coaches didn't seem to know what to do with him. For awhile, they switched him to center. There was even some talk of putting him in a minor-league team to get him used to the punishment that is part of pro hockey.

But in the end, Bobby played defense just as always. And he played for the Bruins.

He helped the team to win the first game of the 1966-67 season, 6-2. In the second game, against Montreal, he scored his first goal on a slap shot from the blue line.

Doug Orr had that puck gold-plated.

He made mistakes, too. More experienced players fooled him with feints. Sometimes he went so deep into the other end that he was caught out of position for the defense. His partner, Gilles Marotte, had to handle a number of rushes all by himself.

Another problem was Bobby's polite, friendly nature. He did not seem to face up to the tough players who try to psych-out rookies with real or imaginary violence.

Wren Blair said: "You must stand up to them, Bobby. Show them that you're willing to fight—and before long they'll stop bothering you. Then your hockey ability can take over."

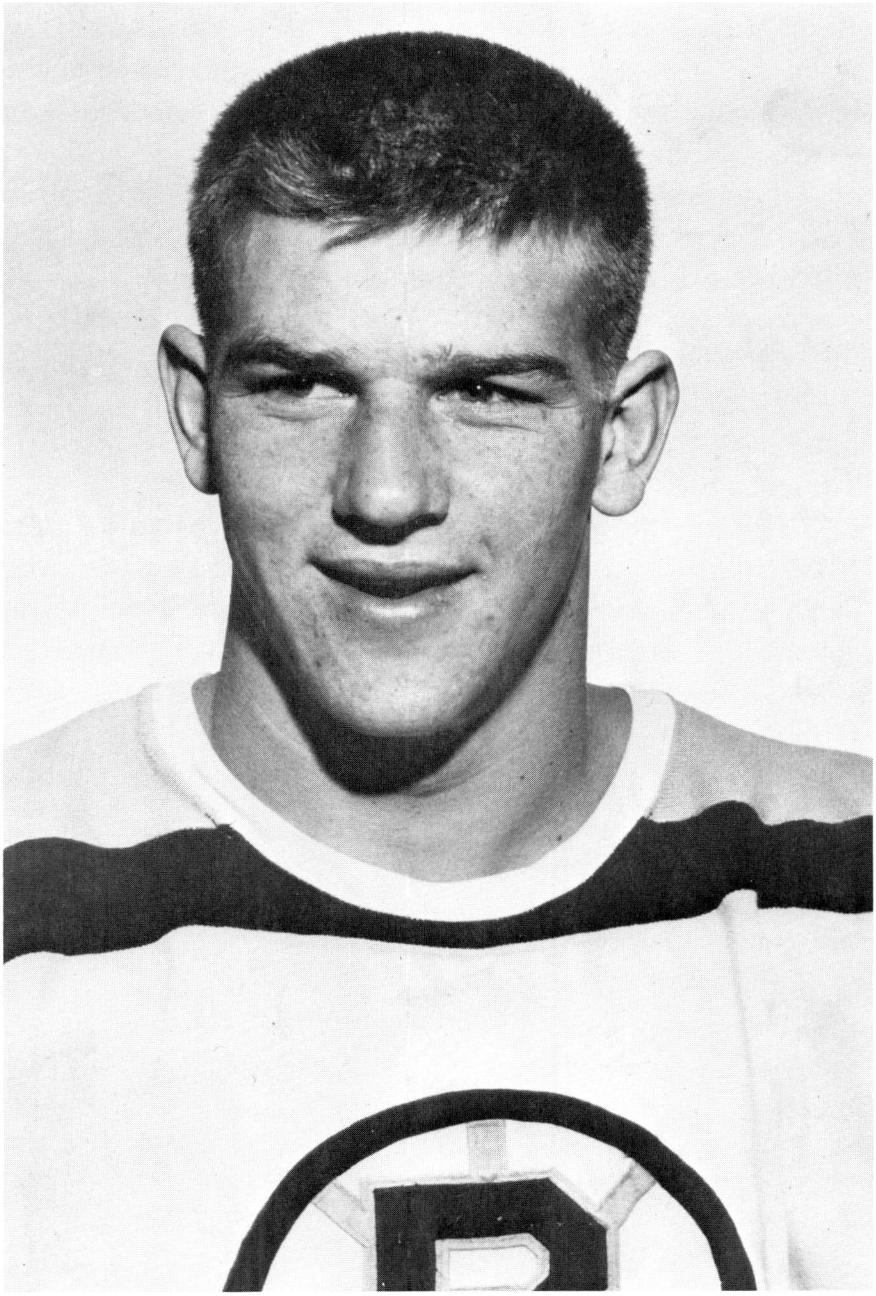

During his first season with the Bruins, Bobby scored 13 goals and made 28 assists. He was selected Rookie of the Year and named to the second All-Star Team.

The rest of the Bruins fared less well. Manager Hap Emms was not skillful in his handling of the players and he made many enemies. The Bruins took out their resentment by playing poorly. Once again, the team finished last.

One disgusted fan shouted: "Hey, Emms! Why don't you trade Bobby Orr? He's making the rest of the team look bad!"

But in the end it was Emms who was eased out. Milt Schmidt, a member of hockey's Hall of Fame, became the new manager of the Bruins. He made several good trades. In one of his best deals, he acquired Phil Esposito, Ken Hodge, and Fred Stanfield from Chicago.

Boston finally began to look like a team with a future.

Bruins coach Harry Sinden congratulates Bobby after a victory over the Toronto Maple Leafs.

In 1967 the NHL expanded from six to twelve. The popularity of the game was booming.

In August, Bobby agreed to play an exhibition game in Winnipeg. It was a benefit for old-time hockey players and Bobby liked to help others. But unfortunately he took a bad fall and injured his right knee. He was in a cast for five weeks and the Bruins' management was furious at their superstar for endangering himself.

Bobby seemed to play better than ever during the first half of the 1967-68 season. In January he shone as defenseman in the All-Star Game, outplaying such hockey giants as Stan Mikita, Bobby Hull, and Gordie Howe.

And the Bruins were heading for the Stanley Cup playoffs for the first time in nine years.

29

The Bruins were contenders for first place when disaster struck. Bobby injured his left knee. He would have to have an operation. For several weeks, he was sidelined. The team began to slip.

Bobby insisted on returning to the ice in March— but by then it was too late to save the Bruins. They finished third. To make matters worse, they lost the East Division playoffs to the Montreal Canadiens, losing four games in a row. Bobby did not score a single goal.

Young fans accompany Bobby to a practice session as he gets back into shape after his knee injury.

Something was still seriously wrong with Bobby's knee. Friends asked about it worriedly when Bobby went to Parry Sound in June to be honored on "Bobby Orr Day."

He revealed that he was going to have to undergo another operation. A few days later he entered a Toronto hospital. Doctors removed a bone chip and said that this time the hockey star should recover completely.

Bobby spent the rest of the summer on crutches. But despite the fact that he had played in only 46 games, with 11 goals and 20 assists, he was awarded the Norris Trophy as outstanding defenseman.

"I didn't deserve it," Bobby said.

The 1969 winners of the NHL top trophies display their awards. *From left:* Bobby Orr, Boston Bruins, Norris Trophy for best defenseman. Phil Esposito, Boston Bruins, Hart Trophy as outstanding NHL player. Danny Grant, Minnesota North Stars, Calder Trophy for rookie of the year. Jacques Plante and Glen Hall, St. Louis Blues, Vezina Trophy for best goal-tending.

In the fall, he worked hard to get the knee into shape. He wanted to make liars out of the people who were saying that Bobby Orr was a "brittle" player, too frail for the rigors of pro hockey.

He came back strongly. The knee held up during crunching bodychecks, high-G maneuvering, and even whacks from enemy woodchoppers' sticks.

With Bobby leading the way, Boston dominated the East Division. Once again, Bobby proved to be the sparkplug of Bruin power. Boston fans began hoping for their first Stanley Cup since 1941.

And then Bobby twisted his bad knee by tripping over a lump on the ice. He was out for only three weeks in February, 1969, but that was enough to cool off the Bruins' pennant momentum.

Once again Montreal clinched the East Division and defeated Boston in the playoffs. It was some consolation when Bobby was voted the Norris Trophy for the second straight year. He had broken two NHL records with his 21 goals and 43 assists.

This time, he could accept the award without feeling guilty.

Bobby is flipped into the air by a body check from Maple Leafs' Rick Ley. Bobby had just fired a goal during a February 1970 game.

It was obvious to all hockey fans that Bobby Orr had joined the ranks of hockey's superstars. What was more, the other Bruins were finally meshing together and looking like champions. The star center, Phil Esposito, predicted that the team would go all the way to the Cup in the 1969-70 season.

Bobby inherited the leadership of the Bruins after veteran Ted Green was sidelined for the season with a head injury. The big, bad Bruins did not resent being captained by a 21-year-old kid. Not when he became the first defenseman in NHL history to win the scoring championship with a total of 120 points.

The Bruins ended the season tied for first place with the Chicago Black Hawks. The rulebooks came out and gave the top slot to the team with the greatest number of victories: Chicago had 45, Boston had only 40.

Bruin stars Bobby Orr and Phil Esposito grin happily after a victory. Bobby's face seems to change in different photographs because of the many bruises and broken noses he has suffered throughout his hockey career.

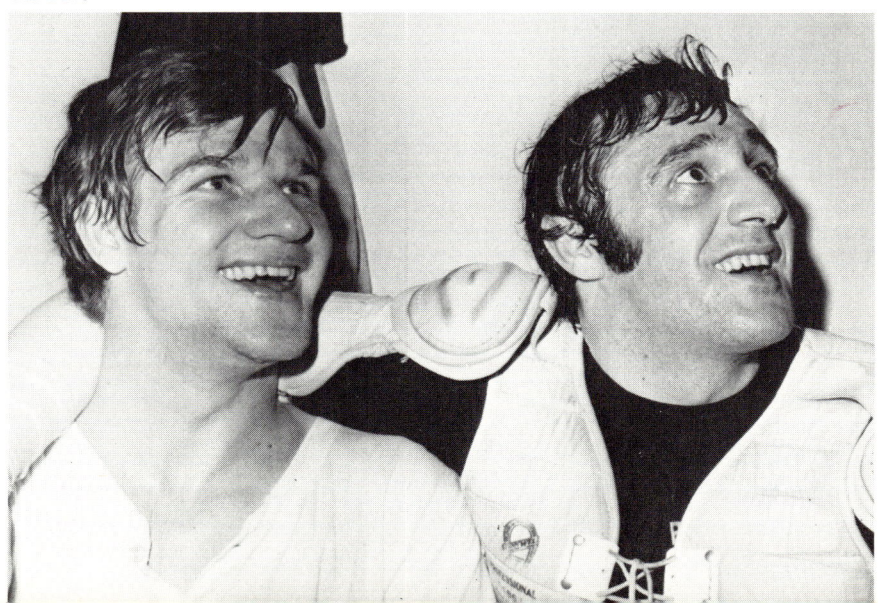

During the second Stanley Cup game, Bobby shoots for goal in the first period. Black Hawk goalie Tony Esposito lies on the ice.

Then it was time for the Stanley Cup playoffs.

Boston met the New York Rangers in the semifinal series. Boston took the first and second games. Then New York took the third and fourth.

Boston won the next two games. New York fans were so outraged that they threw eggs and fruit onto the ice and even set fire to the stands!

In the third game against the Hawks, Tony Esposito had the satisfaction of a caged Bobby Orr. But the Bruins won, 5-2.

Then Boston met Chicago for the Eastern Finals.

It was a real grudge fight, since the Bruins felt they had been "robbed" of first place by the Black Hawks. The star of this series was Bruin Phil Esposito, who accounted for five goals. Boston trampled Chicago four games in a row. Esposito, a former Hawk, played against his own younger brother, Phil, rookie goaltender for Chicago.

37

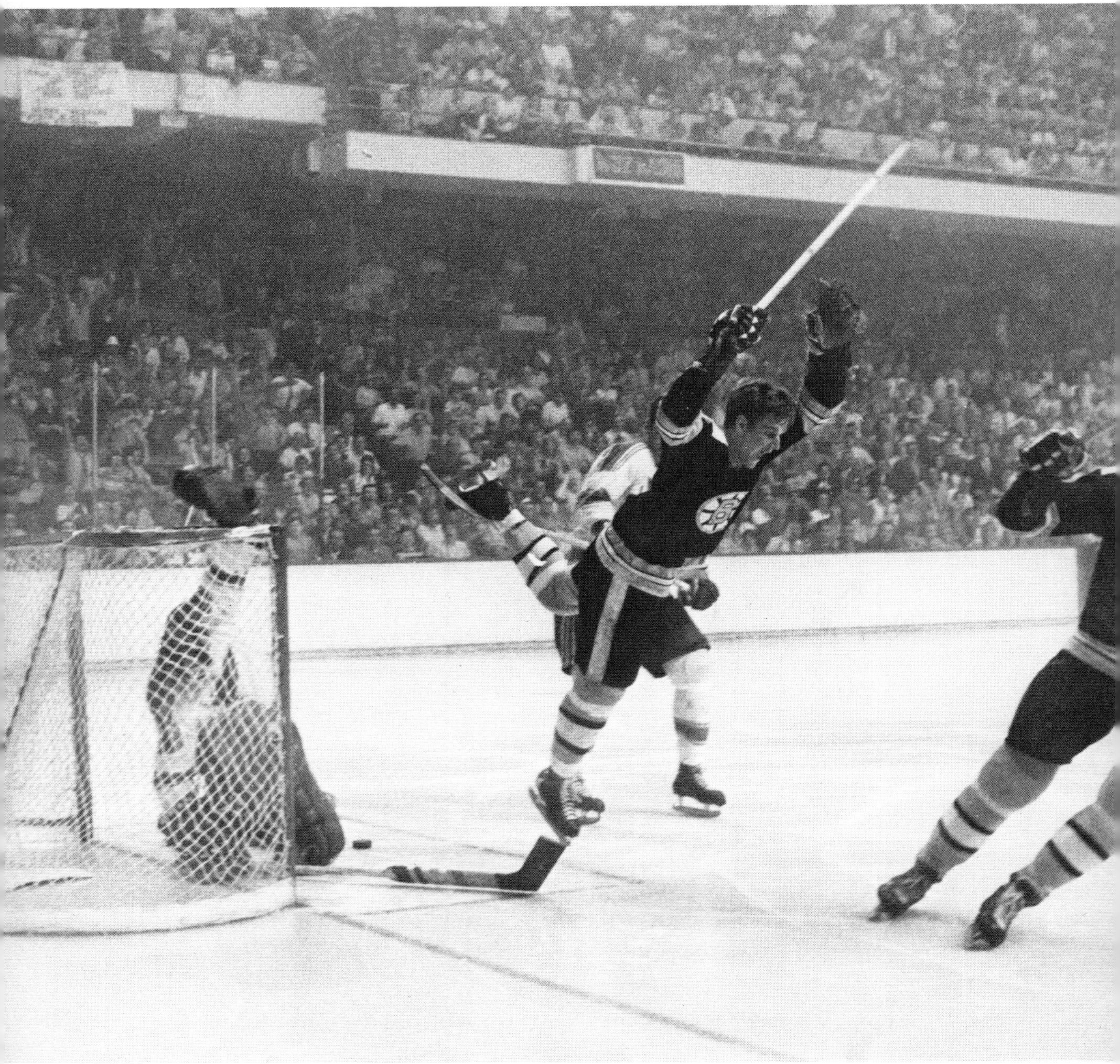

The West Division champs were the St. Louis Blues. As an expansion team, they were not nearly as strong as the old pros from the East.

Nobody was surprised when the Bruins took the first three games, 6-1, 6-2, and 4-1.

The Blues rallied in the fourth game. The last period ended with the score tied, 3-3.

Then Bobby Orr stole the puck. He passed to his center, Derek Sanderson, and streaked for the net. Sanderson fed him a return flip, which Bobby fired between the goalie's legs for the winning score.

A split second later Bobby tripped. The joyous Boston team piled on top of him as he fell. He had clinched the Stanley Cup for Boston.

After scoring the winning goal that clinched the Stanley Cup, Bobby shouts with joy. Not even tripping over a Blues' player's stick can spoil the triumph of the Bruins' first Stanley Cup in 29 years.

Happy crowds thronged the streets of Boston to hail the hockey heroes. *From left:* John Adams, Bobby Orr, Alan Marcote, Bill Speer.

It was their first championship in 29 years. Mobs saluted the team with a victory parade through the streets of Boston. It was a sports fantasy come true: the fans had waited while their Wonder Boy grew up, then watched him work his magic just as they expected him to do.

Bobby Orr was hockey's most honored player that season. He won the Norris Trophy again. He also took the Ross Trophy for leading the NHL in scoring, the Conn Smythe Trophy for most valuable player in Stanley Cup competition, and the Hart Memorial Trophy as most valuable player in the NHL for the 1969-70 season.

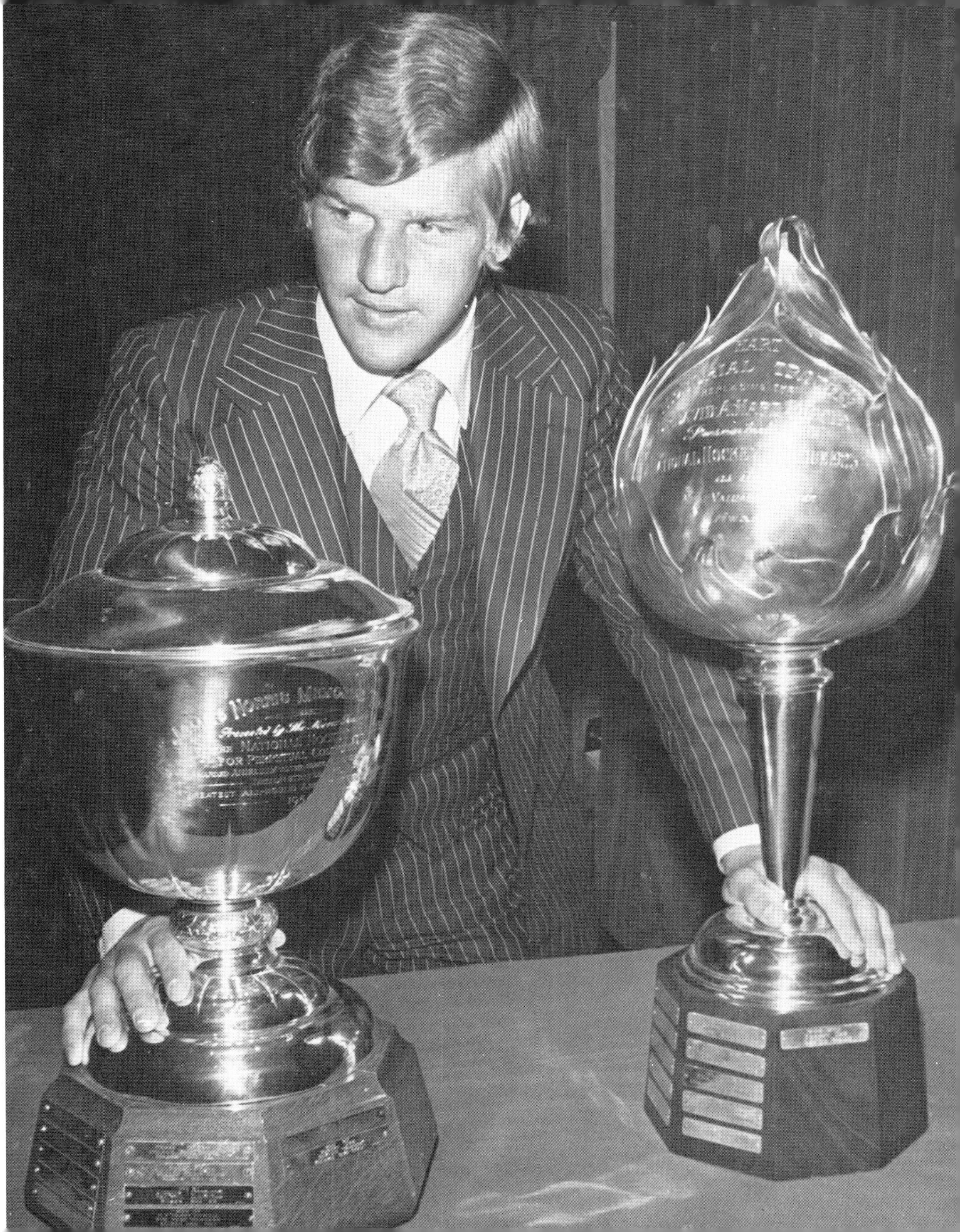

HART

The division title, which had slipped away from the Bruins in 1969-70, finally came their way during the next season.

They nailed down first place easily. Bobby was runner-up in scoring with 37 goals and 139 points. The top man was his team-mate, Phil Esposito. He scored 76 goals—a new NHL season record—and had a total of 152 points.

But disappointment awaited the Bruins in the playoffs. Although they were favored to win, they lost the seven-game series three to four because they were over-confident.

The only bright spot for Boston was a three-goal "hat trick" by Bobby Orr in the fourth game, the first Stanley Cup hat trick by a defenseman in 44 years.

"Just wait until next year!" howled the Bruins.

In a December 1970 game against the North Stars, Bobby came in alone for a shot at the goal. Goalie Gilles Gilbert sent Bobby flying.

Bobby Orr in action against the New York Rangers.

In 1972 the Bruins won the East Division pennant. Bobby Orr's knee gave him trouble from time to time, but he kept playing as well as ever.

In the playoffs, Boston whipped the Toronto Maple Leafs and the St. Louis Blues. Then they defeated the New York Rangers four games to three in a hard-fought series.

In the deciding game, Bobby Orr scored the first goal and set up the second.

The Bruins won, 3-0. Once more they were the top team in professional hockey, winners of the Stanley Cup.

All eyes are on Bobby as he takes the puck past the Bruins' goal during the final Stanley Cup game against the Rangers. Pete Stemkowski *(21)* tries vainly to score. Looking on are Bruins Phil Esposito *(7)* and goalie Ed Johnston.

Bobby Orr married Margaret Louise Wood in 1973.

Bobby Orr has continued to play outstanding hockey. He is easily the best defenseman of all time. But even more, he is one of those rare athletes who make a permanent mark upon their sport. Fans have compared his impact to that of Babe Ruth in baseball or Bill Russell in basketball.

He has set a new standard of excellence. Millions have agreed: after Bobby Orr began to play hockey, the game was never the same again.

Bobby poses with the Stanley Cup, hockey's top award.

ROBERT GORDON ORR

He was born March 20, 1948, in Parry Sound, Ontario, the third of five children of Douglas and Arva Orr. After his discovery by Boston scouts, Bobby was groomed as the "savior" of the Bruins, who waited for him to grow up while publicizing his merits to the patient fans. He was given more publicity than any other young hockey player in history but stayed modest and unspoiled because he played in Canada, far from the Boston spotlight.

He played Junior A hockey for the Oshawa Generals for four seasons, setting many junior records. He joined the Bruins in 1966 and despite injuries, continues to be a mainstay of the team. He is considered the best defenseman of all time.

Bobby married Peggy Wood in a private ceremony in Parry Sound on September 8, 1973. During the off-season, he takes care of several business interests, fishes, hunts, and makes personal appearances for charity. One of his favorite enterprises is a hockey camp for boys that he operates near Orillia, Ontario.

He has written a book of hockey instruction, *Orr on Ice,* in collaboration with Dick Grace.

BOBBY ORR STATISTICS

		Regular Schedule					*Playoffs*				
Season	**Club**	GP	G	A	TP	PIM	GP	G	A	TP	PIM
1966-67	Boston	61	13	28	41	102	—	—	—	—	—
1967-68	Boston	46	11	20	31	63	4	0	2	2	2
1968-69	Boston	67	21	43	64	133	10	1	7	8	10
1969-70	Boston	76	33	87	120	125	14	9	11	20	14
1970-71	Boston	78	37	102	139	91	7	5	7	12	25
1971-72	Boston	76	37	80	117	106	15	5	19	24	19
1972-73	Boston	63	29	72	101	99	5	1	1	2	7
NHL TOTALS		467	181	432	613	719	55	21	47	68	77

Calder Memorial Trophy as outstanding rookie: 1967
Norris Trophy as outstanding defensive player: 1968, 1969, 1970, 1971, 1972, 1973
Hart Trophy as most valuable player: 1970, 1971, 1972
Ross Trophy as leading scorer: 1970
Conn Smythe Trophy as outstanding playoff player: 1970, 1972